THE ACTOR'S GUIDE TO SUCCESS

THE ACTOR'S GUIDE TO SUCCESS

Arthur G. Smith

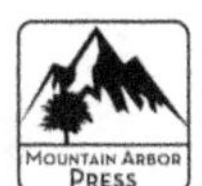

Mountain Arbor
Press

Alpharetta, GA

The Actor's Guide to Success is a work of prescriptive nonfiction (self-help). Although the author has made every effort to ensure the information in this book was correct at the time of first publication, the author does not assume and hereby disclaims any liability to any party for any loss, damage, or disruption caused by errors or omissions, whether such errors or omissions result from negligence, accident, or any other cause. Some names and identifying details have been changed to protect the privacy of individuals.

ISBN: 978-1-63183-880-4 - Paperback

Printed in the United States of America on acid-free paper   0 7 0 2 2 0

∞ This paper meets the requirements of ANSI/NISO Z39.48-1992 (Permanence of Paper)

Grateful acknowledgment is made to the following for reprint of previously published material:

James Clear: Excerpt from "The Myth and Magic of Deliberate Practice" by James Clear, copyright © James Clear. Reprinted by permission of James Clear.

Lyrics from "Boss" by Shawn Carter, Tyrone William Griffin, Dernst "D'Mile" Emile II, and Beyoncé Knowles-Carter. Copyright © 2018 Carter Boys Music, Oakland 13 Music, These are Pulse Songs, BMG Platinum Songs, EMI Blackwood Music Inc., and Copyright Control. All rights on behalf of Carter Boys Music and Oakland 13 Music administered by WC Music Corp. Dawg Music Administered by WC Music Corp. Reprinted by permission of Alfred Music and Hal Leonard LLC.

www.theactorsguidetosuccess.com
www.agsmediainc.com
www.powertalkglobal.com

Cover artwork © 2020 by Christopher Wardlaw

To Sallie, my mother, for your infinite love and support.

To my mentors, Solomon and Brother Paul, for your perpetual guidance and communal wisdom. To Khalid, my son, for your growth and maturity.

And to Alexandria, for being a genuine friend when I most needed it.

CONTENTS

FOREWORD

One of my favorite quotes is, "Talent is the constant desire to practice."

I've had the privilege of working in casting for the past thirteen years, and I think one of the best ways to practice is to be consistently learning. I've always been an advocate of actors continuously remaining a student of their craft. That's one of the biggest reasons why I'm excited to write this foreword. When Arthur told me that he was writing this book, I knew it would be an excellent tool for all actors and artists looking to thrive! Arthur has had great success managing and representing actors, and I'm thrilled that he's put some of those lessons and principles into this book!

Arthur's straight-to-the-point approach is very much needed in the acting arena. So often, we focus on the craft and the technical aspects of mastering a performance, but we don't consider how vital the "mindset business" is to actors' and artists' success! I particularly love the chapter about playing out the end before the beginning. So many actors want success but have not detailed what a successful acting career looks like for them. Following the steps in this book will help you rethink your approach to acting and your artistic career.

This book contains keys that are not only principles for

actors, but these are principles for LIFE. I know that one of the keys to succeeding as an actor is leading a full, balanced, and purposeful life. I'm grateful that Arthur took the time to write this book, and I pray that this book sets you on a path of breakthroughs, bookings, and blessings!

—Rhavynn Drummer
Head of Casting, Tyler Perry Studios

PREFACE

I was inspired to write this book after reading Grant Cardone's *The Millionaire Booklet: How to Get Super Rich*. If you have not read it, I strongly encourage you to do so, especially if you, like me, aspire to be super-rich. That booklet recommends ten basic principles to becoming a millionaire or multimillionaire, whichever you prefer!

One of the fundamental principles mentioned in the booklet is the ability and willingness to help people. "If you want to make a billion dollars, simply help a billion people," Grant states. What a profound statement. I thought about that for days on end: What is it that I can offer people to help them? And then it occurred to me that my greatest strength lies in my ability to lead and inspire people! It is in that spirit that this book is written. I love helping people achieve their objectives, and I especially enjoy assisting creatives.

More on that shortly.

When I was approximately twelve years old, growing up in Atlanta, my father committed suicide. He was a Vietnam War veteran and suffered PTSD from the effects of Agent Orange. My mother, an educator, and a newly single mom, sought out various community organizations for my brother and me to be involved. She chose the Atlanta graduate chapter of Alpha Phi Alpha Fraternity, Inc. to help guide us. One particular weekend Darryl M. Bell, an actor from the NBC sitcom *A Different World* and member of the fraternity, came to address one of the leadership classes held for our group. He talked about the pursuit of one's goals in the face of adversity. His message moved me, and it changed my world. He signed my March of Dimes hat, which I still have to this day, and I credit that moment, in no small part, to pointing me toward a career in entertainment.

Years later, I started my talent management company, AGS Media. I count this as one of my greatest joys in life. Helping a first-time actor book a feature film, or having an industry veteran land a lead role in a TV show, is of equal importance to me. Suffice it to say that I love being a talent manager in the entertainment industry. So, if you are unfamiliar with what a talent manager is or does, please watch the television show *Entourage*. Try to view the entire series, but, minimally, check out a few episodes from season one. The character Eric "E." Murphy, remarkably played by Kevin Connolly, personifies the job to a tee.

As a talent manager, one of my roles is to help clients establish strategic directions to think beyond a particular moment while not disappearing from the experiences of that moment, be they good, bad, or indifferent. The entertainment industry, much like life, is often met with failure, and temporary disappointment, even for established or "named" actors. But there are lots of highs too! One must be willing to experience both.

I'm particularly sympathetic to helping women, people

of color, and underrepresented voices. I certainly want to help them break into the entertainment business, but I am confident the principles and strategies in this book, properly applied, will work for anyone.

As Shawn Carter, my favorite musician, once rhymed, "Over here, we measure success by how many people successful next to you/Here we say you're broke if everybody is broke except for you! Boss!"

My goal for aspiring creatives is to:

1. Help you understand how the entertainment business operates
2. Help you perfect your craft
3. Help you accomplish your objectives of starting and maintaining a career in the entertainment industry

Equally important, I want to help you to be great! So, let's go!

INTRODUCTION

This book will give you some tools and a road map for your journey, from the mindset you must have to the execution of auditioning and the actual preparation it takes to achieve your goals. It is intentionally concise. Partly because the fundamentals of success are simple, and if you learn those, you, too, will increase the likelihood of achievement. I have always believed in being straightforward. For example, I admire people like Stephen A. Smith and Dr. Michael Eric Dyson, who wax poetic and turn a simple yes or no answer into a thirty-minute dissertation. It is awe-inspiring . . . but it is just not my style.

There are very few African-American talent managers in the entertainment industry who represent writers, actors, or directors. I know, or least have met, most of them, and they are incredible leaders. A few who come to mind are E. Brian Dobbins, who manages Anthony Anderson, Tracee Ellis Ross, and Kenya Barris, amongst others; Jerome Martin, who currently manages Kofi Siriboe and is also responsible for managing a significant portion of Tyrese Gibson's career; Mikael Moore, who works with Janelle Monáe; and the incomparable James "JL" Lassiter, who represents Will Smith.

Although the above talent managers are African-Americans, the other managers whose work I am incredibly impressed with, Dany Garcia, who manages Dwayne Johnson and Henry Cavill, and Dave Becky, who manages Kevin Hart, Issa Rae, et al., are two of them. And Jeff Morrone, who represents Gabrielle Union, Dania Ramirez, Meagan Good, et al., is one of the most helpful managers you'd ever want to know.

And here, I want to be clear: I am not those guys or woman, in Dany's case. They have bigger rosters, substantive revenues, and well-documented, public profiles.

So why should you listen to me? One, because I have the willingness to help you. And two, I know what I speak.

It has been a journey.

My first "office" was the Morrison Regional branch of the Charlotte Mecklenburg Public Library. I was just starting and didn't have the cash to secure a formal office, so I made the library my office. I owned a laptop, but one day dropped it in a rush, so I had to use the public computer terminals on the second floor as "my office computer." Looking back on it, the library was the first co-working space well before WeWork, Knotel, or The Gathering Spot. And Charlie, the librarian, would often open the downstairs conference room so I could make calls and not disturb other library patrons.[1]

At that time, I was working with local talent and would try and pitch or follow up on self-taped auditions. Los

---

[1] By the way, a portion of this book's proceeds will go the Charlotte Mecklenburg Public Library. It's my way of saying thank you!

Angeles–based casting directors (CDs) would never return my calls. To remedy that, I ordered two new cell phones, one with a New York City area code and phone number, which I still have to this day, and one with a Los Angeles area code and phone number. I would phone New York City casting directors from my Los Angeles number and Los Angeles–based casting directors from my New York City number! Suddenly, people started to phone me back!

What I am pointing out here is the importance of being tenacious and creative. Like the great Carthaginian general Hannibal said, "We will either find a way or make one." So take note.

This past year, I have tripled the movie quote of one client while adding a first-time "executive producer" credit to their résumé. I also signed a twenty-year industry veteran and secured another client a brand deal that eclipses their movie quote.

The fascinating aspect, I am doing this from Atlanta, not Los Angeles or New York City. Again, I am not suggesting I am at the top of the heap—far from it. But I'm a long way from the public library.

CHAPTER 1
WHERE DO I START?

Success is the progressive realization of your goals. Progressive being the operative word.

—Solomon Majid

Here is what you must first understand. Greatness is not taught in school. Skills are taught in school. Greatness is achieved via countless hours of perfecting your craft and assimilating the lessons of scene study, voice mastery, body and breath control, and facial movement. Proficiency, rudiment, and nuance are instructed in classes. They are perfected through repetitive application. Know the difference.

There is no shortcut to greatness or success. You may achieve fame in an instant. But impact comes from the sheer result of dedication and commitment to practice. Yes, practice (Allen Iverson voice[2]).

I had a client once tell me that she does not need acting classes. Just keep her working, and she will be okay, she commented. No wonder her TV show got canceled after only one season—every person of impact practices. LeBron James, a seventeen-year NBA veteran, spends hours in the gym before and after games. And his summer workouts are notoriously intense. Drake, while in the middle of a global music tour, travels his singing coach with him so he can keep his voice sharp. Virgil Abloh, at the height of his career, perfects his craft through an incredible work ethic. These are masters.

Perfect your craft. Always. Constantly. Become a master.

Pick a dojo. Master your craft.

Now, to be sure, some dojos are better than others. If you're a high school student considering college, New York University's Tisch School of the Arts, Howard University's Department of Theatre Arts, and Yale's School of Drama are just a few that have profound records of producing top-notch creatives. There are many more.

As a talent manager, I'm often asked, what's the best acting method? To quote Nasir Jones, "Ain't no best—East, West, North, South." (He was referring to rappers, but the point is the same.) The best acting method is the one that's true for you.

---

2 Look up "Allen Iverson practice" on Google.

The acting coach you select is a personal decision. It's akin to choosing a marriage or business partner.

Here is a process to help you to identify a coach you want. Take a piece of paper and draw a line down the middle. On the left side, write a list of the top ten characteristics and skills you want to learn, which are most important to you, and on the other side, write a list of the top ten things that you don't want or will not tolerate. Don't forget to put a date on it so that when you look back to review the goals sheet, you can have a point of reference. As a minor point, always document your objectives. You want a record of your progress so you can measure it. When you have finished your list, place the paper on your bathroom mirror, or in another visible location, and review it daily.

Then, using the guidelines you created, you are ready to start looking for an acting coach. Seek feedback from others about their experiences and ask them probing questions, but the ultimate deciding factors should be based on the characteristics and skills you want to learn. Next, audit the coach's classes, if they allow you to, and evaluate them before you enroll. This technique could also apply to other areas of your life.[3]

Now, to answer the question at the start of the chapter: "Where do I start?" The first place you start is with yourself.

It seems such a simple answer. Here is why: When you

---

[3] This decision technique is also known as The Benjamin Franklin Close or "The Balance Sheet Close."

are in the middle of a litany of no's, struggling to receive a callback, and on the verge of giving up on your career, you have to be able to look inward, without being hopelessly introverted, to find your purpose and real why. It will help you to remain steadfast and confident. Once you reach that point, the point of certainty, you are one step closer to accomplishing your objective. Most people look for the point of validation—booking a role, for example—as a tipping point. But that is *not* the tipping point; instead, that is the manifestation of the tipping point. The exact tipping point is the moment of your decision point of certainty. In fact, before anyone else believes it, you must believe it for yourself. And your belief has to be unshakable, because it *will* get tested.

Start by writing down your "why." Your purpose. Your chief definite aim around your creative pursuits—use Google to search for Bruce Lee's "My Definite Chief Aim" as a guide and template for creating your own.[4]

And again, date it, and post it in a place where you can look at it every day.

The first thing I do when I onboard new clients, especially those new to having management, is to give them a book list and have them read every book on the agenda during the first six months I begin working with them. It serves

---

[4] The concept of Definite Chief Aim is best explained in *Think and Grow Rich* by Napoleon Hill.

a dual purpose. If they are unwilling to read preparation material so that they can mentally prepare their minds, then they are likely not cut out for the entertainment industry, or the sheer number of no's they will face. Two, if persons are unwilling to commit to growing, to becoming their best selves, I immediately have to look for a compelling reason to work with them long term.

A quick pop culture reference. You may recall MTV's *Making the Band 2* episode where Sean Combs asked the contestants, all artists, to walk twelve and a half miles from Manhattan to Brooklyn to get him a slice of Junior's cheesecake. Not only because he desired some cheesecake, but he also wanted to instill a sense of the level of commitment, focus, and work ethic one must have to succeed as an artist on his label. Please take a good look at that to apply the lesson to yourself.

The point is . . . start walking (P. Diddy voice)! Not to Junior's, but toward your goals!

That said, after you have selected the style of coach that you respond well to and that also pushes you to be better, you must do the work.

I can relate this differently. Most recently, I started a new venture in the tech world. Recently, I founded PowerTalk, a celebrity education technology platform to teach college students soft skills. At the beginning of the year, I began taking classes at ATDC, a start-up incubator at Georgia Tech that helps technology entrepreneurs in Georgia launch and build successful companies. The program starts with a class called Customer Discovery led by an extraordinary man, Bill Hogan. The classes are ridiculously inexpensive, $25 every three months, but the information is supremely valuable and the mentors who advise you who have sold businesses north of a combined $500,000,000. The incubator has a 90 percent success rate, whereas, on the flip side, most startups have a 90 percent likelihood of failure. Think about that. Who would not want to learn from them? I sure did. Yet, six months later, out of the group of people who started in the same class as me, there were only two persons who finished with me.

The point is, people give up. They offer all manner of excuses. They say it's too complicated, or life happens, or they face too many personal demons. Or they encounter an obstacle too tough to handle, and they decide that the barrier is more significant than their desire for success. Some just simply change their minds. What I want you to see here is this: you have chosen this path as your profession, or whatever it is that you want to accomplish, the key is to keep going. *No matter what.*

Back to ATDC. As a part of customer discovery, one exercise we had to do was to interview prospective customers. And since my potential customers are college students, I was in the sweltering Atlanta heat and humidity, during the middle of summer, with temperatures often exceeding ninety degrees Fahrenheit, interviewing hundreds of college students at Atlanta-area college campuses. We were required to interview ten persons a week. One particular week I decided that I wanted to push myself, and I conducted fifty-two interviews. When I went back to present, my prior week one mentor pulled me aside, and said, "Arthur, I don't believe I've ever seen a founder with as much drive as you. I look forward to reading about you in the *Wall Street Journal* one day." So know this, your tenacity will get you recognized—for sure.

That is the level of commitment one has to have to be competitive.

At this point in reading this book, you are now entering the "get it done" level. And before you can get it done, you, and you alone, have to think that you can.

So, again, to answer the question of "where do you start?" It's with yourself and your state of mind. So, pause reading for a moment, review the book list at the end, and order each of the books. And, if you are unable to order the books, go to your nearest public library and obtain them there.

An earned secret: If you follow these steps, when you begin training in preparation to audition, you will be much more prepared than your fellow actors. They will feel it, and most importantly, you will know it.[5]

---

[5] I once heard Chris Lyons, from Andreessen Horowitz, speak about his investment philosophy and the concept of investing with founders who have earned secrets. I've been borrowing the phrase ever since!

CHAPTER 2
PLOT OUT THE
END IN THE BEGINNING

Never send to know for whom the bell tolls; it tolls for thee.

—John Donne

The questionnaire in this chapter is designed to help evaluate talent and brand partnerships. It was created by a friend of mine, who, at the time, was an executive for one of the most impactful hip-hop music managers turned CEO, and now entertainment mogul and music legend, Russell Simmons. I utilize it as an onboarding process to evaluate prospective clients and whether our objectives are aligned. I include it here for you to use as a guide to your creative goals.

As a side note, if your current management is not using some process-driven method to guide your career, or can't speak to the process, then you should critically evaluate your relationship. Why? More often than not, it is highly likely that they do not have a process! Now, to be sure, one of the most critical methods one can utilize is the power of relationships, and it took me a time to understand the gravity of that, which I'm still learning. More on that shortly.

Two quick points about plotting out a career path: One, you must start with an end goal in mind so you can gauge where you are on your road to success. And again, two, you must always keep your "why" at the forefront of your mind, which is your purpose. If your mission is to help inspire others, then include that while writing your Definite Chief Aim. If your goal is to be famous, state that too.

I am not seeking to evaluate your purpose, only to offer you a guide to achieve it.

The questionnaire is below:

What are your overall objectives for this year? The following year?

Who has been your most loyal fan/consumer? Do you have any data or research you can share around your target consumer?

What have you identified as your biggest challenge?

What has worked well for you in the past when targeting your biggest fans? What hasn't worked so well?

Who is in your competitive landscape? Who would you consider your direct competitor?

What is your current portfolio of products?

What has your portfolio of products been for the last twelve months? What will you produce in the next eighteen months?

What areas, and in what demographics, would you like to see more name and brand recognition?

Are you open to co-branded opportunities? Who would you consider to be a parallel brand?

What potential partnerships would you like to cultivate this year?

Do you have a brand position statement? What is your brand position?

Where do you want to see your brand? One year? Three years? Five years?

If applicable, where globally is your product sold?

What is your specific objective of working with companies?

In addition to my work with actors, I also have a background in corporate America and have worked with several brands on their celebrity-engagement strategies. Once, I accompanied a company client to a retail giant. In the meeting, the executive asked my client a simple question. He requested my magazine client to succinctly explain if he were a customer walking by the magazine stand, who would be to the left of them, and who would be to the right.

In that same context, think of yourself as a magazine brand. Who is to the left of you? Who is to the right? Doing so will contextualize your objectives as a benchmark for what your peers are achieving. And notice I said peers. It may be ideal to think of Will Smith and Denzel Washington as persons adjacent to you, but until they become peers—which means you're a global box office star—then you should select someone in your direct sphere. How will you know who your peers are? You'll spot them from auditions and acting classes.

After you complete the questionnaire, print it out and post it someplace where you can readily access it. Read it every morning after you wake up and every night before you go to sleep. Internalize the answers; those are your road map. Use those answers to guide your decision-making process and your journey.

After all, people think in pictures. And again, before you can achieve it, you must see it. Always remember, the first level of creation is in your mind. The second level of creation is in the physical universe.[6]

---

[6] Mandela Schumacher-Hodge Dixon, CEO of Founder Gym, eloquently conveyed this during a training program I once participated in, and she appropriately credited Stephen Covey from his highly acclaimed book, *The 7 Habits of Highly Effective People.*

CHAPTER 3
BE EXCELLENT

Make it happen or make excuses, but you can't do both.

—Bobby Rio

How does one achieve excellence? It's a straightforward concept, although it may not be easy to accomplish. The fundamentals of excellence boil down to two keys: commitment and preparation. The time it may take you to achieve your creative objectives may or may not be fast. No one knows that, and anyone who says that they do is speculating, offering an anecdotal viewpoint, or being dishonest. You should be prepared for as long as it takes to achieve it.

If it happens fast, so be it. If it takes longer, that's okay. The real question is, how long are you willing to work to achieve your objectives? That is something only you can and should answer, which is why it is so important to be specific about your Definite Chief Aim. Notice that Bruce Lee had a specific timeline for his objectives. You should too. Be as definitive as possible (e.g. I want to star in the remake of *Pretty Woman* by 2024).

This philosophy is not intended for you only to meditate, think positively, and expect things to happen. It's not that kind of party. I don't advocate that. Some do, but I am not one of those persons.

Is it because success is preordained for a few, well-connected actors? No. A close and unbiased investigation will reveal such assertions to be false beliefs. The critical factor is to persevere.[7]

Get known where you are. There are successful actors in Tokyo, Shanghai, Lagos, and Johannesburg. However, I would advise moving to the closest primary film market that you can, one where you can increase the likelihood of being known. But make no mistake, some reps and producers will spend their time searching for you, no matter where you live, especially if you have built a reputation of creating work of impact.

The *Art* book, listed on the recommendation list at the end of this book, offers a dynamic explanation of what makes good art: technical expertise itself adequate to produce an emotional impact. You have to be technically

---

[7] "The genius thing that we did was we didn't give up" (Shawn Carter).

sound. How does one become technically sound? You practice. You make mistakes. You flub lines. You break character. But you do it again. And again. And again. And again.

To illustrate, when I was in high school, I ran track and my track coach, Richard Prince, made us focus on the fundamentals of arm movement and hip placement. I used to hate doing those particular sets of drills, and I often wondered how this was going to make me faster. Oddly enough, the better I did the exercises and turned my hands over more quickly, the quicker my feet would move, and my times would incrementally improve. What Coach Prince was doing was instilling technical expertise into our lives as runners. That is the point of all coaching: to develop and train you toward technical expertise. By the way, our 4x400 team, where I ran the anchor leg, set a school record as a result of those drills. So Coach Prince knew exactly what he was doing!

There is a concept called deliberate practice you should also know, not merely in name but actuality. George "Shotgun" Shuba, twice a teammate to Jackie Robinson, with the Montreal Royals and the Brooklyn Dodgers, demonstrated it well:

Once, a journalist was interviewing Shuba at his residence and asked him what it felt like to be such a natural hitter. Without saying a word, he took the reporter downstairs. In the shadows of the basement, Shuba picked up a bat and began to repeat a series of practice swings. Before each swing, he would call out a particular pitch such as "fastball, low and away" or "slider, inside" and adjust his approach accordingly.

Once he finished the routine, Shuba set the bat down, picked up a piece of chalk, and scratched a tally mark on the wall. Then he flicked on the lights to reveal thousands of tally marks covering the basement walls. Reportedly, Shuba then looked at the journalist and said, "Don't you ever tell me that I'm a natural hitter again."[8]

The point is that you must practice so much that people perceive you as a "natural." Where? Wherever you can! In the mirror. At a community theater. At your acting coach's studio. Wherever you can.

Now that you've created your list and identified your coach, you must display a *willingness* to be coached and to do the work necessary for you to grow. You must *commit* yourself to growth and the training process of enhancement.

When I was in college, I was elected student body president during my junior year. It was a lot of fun, and I had to give an incredible amount of speeches. Near the beginning

---

[8] This story is reprinted from James Clear's blog, "The Myth and Magic of Deliberate Practice."

of the semester, I spoke at convocation alongside the head football coach, Bill Hayes, a towering figure and a motivator to no end.

After my speech, Dr. Dorothy J. Harris, the student government association advisor, walked up to me and said, "Arthur, that was profound! The entire faculty could feel your energy. You are a natural!" Little did she know, moments after I was elected, I spent the summer practicing by reading various speeches from Dr. Martin Luther King Jr. and Malcolm X in the mirror. In fact, as a freshman, I won a scholarship from the Charlotte alumni chapter of Kappa Alpha Psi Fraternity, Inc., through my reading of Malcolm in his famous speech, "The Ballot or the Bullet."

I stared into the mirror and would practice their cadences and command of language. I would envision the day when I was giving speeches, mastering oration, and speaking in front of large crowds.

Here is the backstory. When I was a rising senior in high school, I spent the summer interning for INROADS, a developmental program for top high school students of color who would work well in corporate America. To graduate, we had to give a speech in front of our classmates. I was so nervous that I walked in, saw my high school crush in the front row, and said, "Hi, my name is . . ." Let's call her Angela "Queen" Johnson.

The entire auditorium burst out laughing, and I was so embarrassed. That whole year, my homeboys, as a practical joke, would call my house and ask for "Angela" and then hang up laughing. Finally, my mother got wind of the prank and asked me, "Why are these kids calling here and asking for Angela?"

I had to explain to her what happened and she said, "Well, it seems to me, you're well on your way to being a fabulous speaker."

I replied in frustration, "Why do you say that?"

She said, "Because you now know what not to do. Plus, now, you know your name!"

My ultimate point is this: Practice. Practice. Practice. Practice deliberately. And keep practicing.[9]

Some additional steps:

Determine your ideal scene or ideal state (you develop this by writing your Definite Chief Aim, vision board, or something similar). You have to be specific and definite. (My definition of Ideal Scene is this: a picture in your mind of a perfect situation, without spot or blemish; absolute perfection.)

What exactly are you doing to accomplish your ideal scene?

What books are you reading to increase your knowledge skill sets?

Who are you surrounding yourself with to help push your goals forward?

Who is giving you advice?

---

[9] Malcolm Gladwell references the ten-thousand-hour rule in his book *Outliers*. His ultimate point is natural ability requires a huge investment of time in order to materialize.

Evaluate these questions, honestly and openly, every six months and then watch what happens.

CHAPTER 4
AM I READY FOR MANAGEMENT?

Whole time I was ready, they was like "Hold up, wait a minute" and I was "Nah, let's get it."
—Aubrey Drake Graham

What does a manager actually do? A manager's primary duty is to serve as the intermediary between the talent and the business ecosystem. But, like any dynamic relationship, the relationship between a manager and talent can be redefined to mean whatever the parties like. For example, some managers serve as the right hand to the talent or actor. Then some managers read every script to identify projects that may interest the actor. Like any relationship, you should define it and be clear about expectations. And you do that over time.

Regardless of the actual job, your manager should be adding value to you by offering an honest assessment of the marketplace. And you should add value to them by listening and heeding their viewpoint, as they have a vested interest in your growth and success. And they should undoubtedly build relationships on your behalf. A manager-talent connection should be based on trust, responsibility, and knowingness—knowing what you are after and vice versa.

A quick comment on pay. The industry standard for talent management fees for actors is a 10 percent commission. Some managers, based on the amount of work, may charge more for new talent, but it should not exceed 15 percent. I have read of some managers charging upward to 25 percent commission, and that, in my view, is beyond the pale. The same goes for agents, who, in California, are regulated by the Talent Agencies Act of 1978, SAG-AFTRA Franchise Agreements, and the California Labor Commission to 10 percent commission of a client's earnings. If you have questions for what is commissionable, do a Google search for "SAG-AFTRA's What is Commissionable?" and read the SAG-AFTRA link that pops up.

Again, one of the reasons it is so important to be well-read is so that you can understand the business aspect of entertainment too. For example, in California and New York, talent managers are prohibited from solely procuring work for their clients. However, it happens as a matter of practice. I am also aware of scenarios where A-list talent directly employs managers as executives of their production companies. Still, those arrangements are unique and based on the high demands of the talent.

So, do you need a manager? Well, that depends on you and your Definite Chief Aim. If your objective is to be a local, working actor and you are not intent on building a global brand, you are less likely to need a manager; but again, that is relative. Some managers will shepherd local talent. I am not one of them. I have always thought the way to have the most significant impact is to impact the greatest. And when I look back on my managing career, every step of the way, I have managed talent of increasingly significant impact and those who are intent on becoming a global brand.

Some people do need managers, but if you are starting, you should first focus on being proficient. I am not going to expound on how to obtain a manager because two of the books on the recommended book list speak to the process of securing a manager, but I will offer you a few nuggets.

- Using the Benjamin Franklin Close method, you should identify the characteristics you want in a manager.
- Attend local actor showcases.
- Network and build relationships with managers and agents.

For example, if a manager you have been seeking out is speaking or having a public appearance, then make your way to attend and introduce yourself. Follow up with a "Nice to meet you" email the next business day. If you need to know where to obtain email addresses, go to www.findthatlead.com or try phoning their office and asking their assistant where you may send a query email too. Also, be very kind to the assistants; they can be of extreme importance to you.

When the market demand for your services or your potential market demand, a very subjective measurement for sure, exceeds your ability to manage singlehandedly, then you are ready for a manager. Until that happens, put your head down and continue to practice and to work.

Once you secure a manager, you should speak with your manager at least once every two weeks. When some immediate business is happening, conversations should occur more frequently. I know some managers don't like returning calls, but it is good to keep in touch, if for nothing more than a quick check-in. And don't always rely on them to call you. Call them! If they don't return phone calls, that should tell you exactly what they think of your relationship. Have you ever not returned a phone call to someone of importance to you?

CHAPTER 5
THE BIGGEST SECRET IN ENTERTAINMENT

*One of the deep secrets of life is that all that is
really worth the doing is what we do for others.*
—Lewis Carroll

When I was starting as a manager, one of the hardest tasks I had was to convince clients used to doing things on their own that they should trust me. It is one thing being in the position of manager, but quite another for them to trust the manager to add value.

As an actor, when you are first starting, it is just you and your sheer desire. You are your most prominent advocate and, naturally, your biggest cheerleader, which is good because such is the requirement for one to succeed. The growth challenge occurs when you operate off the "it's just me" philosophy, and it becomes challenging to expand unless you are intentional about growing. It is the difference between a local eatery and a national chain or a mom-and-pop store and a start-up, which, by definition, is a scalable business. If you intend to grow to become globally recognized, then you must have a business process for that growth.

Tony Robbins said it best: "Success leaves clues." Clue number one, the most successful actors in the world have layers of reps. And the greatest of those have teams of people to support the growth of their brands.

Why is that? Because they understand the secret.

LeBron James has Maverick Carter, Jamal Henderson, and a team of people who implement business processes. Common has the inimitable Derek Dudley, and Leonardo DiCaprio has Rick Yorn.

These are brilliant business minds who rival the creative capacity of their talent and CEOs of multinational corporations.

If you are intent on becoming a huge brand, then find a person, using proven business principles, who is capable of scaling your brand. And that is a process, not an event.

One of my former clients was a political commentator and popular urban talk show host. He was so used to booking his own appearances that I had to sit him down and explain that while that process may have worked while he was a solo practitioner, it will not work if he wants to grow.

So here is the secret:

Content is king, but process is senior to content.

You must have a process for growing your brand—not just a method for creating content.

What is your process for scaling or growing as a brand? Having a workable process at hand is critical if you want to scale. Some people want to scale but don't want to employ people. That is counterproductive and not wise.

It is grueling, but sometimes you may have to sacrifice family and personal commitments. Similarly, you will have to invest money back into the growth of your brand.

So, again, that is a decision you and you alone have to make.

Last example. Beyoncé employs forty-plus persons, and Steve Pamon, the CEO of her company, is one of the smartest people in entertainment. Her leadership team makes up some of the kindest people you would ever want to meet. They embody her brand and brand values. Let that serve as success clue number two as you build out your brand: be kind.

One last thought about "the process." Throughout your journey, you will experience many no's. Please do not internalize being told no, and do not take it personally. You have to realize that every instance of being told no is outside of your control. Your total focus should be on controlling your thoughts to determine your impact, because the quality of your thoughts determines your scale of impact. Guard against negative thinking, even when it appears things are not going your way. As a creator, you are a creative center, and your mind and its thoughts are the single most crucial aspects of creation.

And once you complete an audition, let go of any anticipated outcomes. That is to say, don't worry about the project, whether you booked it or not. You will drive yourself crazy if you don't!

Take a lesson from Tiger Woods, who reportedly learned at an early age to compartmentalize his thinking. He did not break his golf club over his knee if he made a lousy shot or enjoy a great shot beyond a roaring fist-pump. In either case, Tiger let go of each result after each ball.

If you allow the temporary no's to overwhelm you, it will have a spillover effect and impact your relationships, your sanity, and the overall state of mind. You have to have the internal leadership and the attitude of never regretting yesterday and the realization that life is in today, and *you* make your tomorrow. And so you do.

CHAPTER 6
THE POWER OF FAILURE IS SUCCESS

*Success is not something that happens to you;
it's something that happens because of you and
because of the actions you take.*

—Grant Cardone

Failure is the most significant building block in the universe. Why? Because if you are motivated to improve, you will do just that. Your deficiencies will serve as the litmus test for your success.

How?

Very simply. I will illustrate . . .

I recently had a coffee meeting with a young actor after a talk that I gave. I wanted to get her viewpoint about some of the challenges that she faces so that I can write from the perspective of a young actor.

A quick note about viewpoint: Life is ultimately about consideration. If you are an actor portraying a role, essentially you are operating out a perspective of what life is like in the eyes of that character. Consider the viewpoint of a producer or casting director. If you are a producer and you are hiring for a particular role or character, which would you select, someone who is marginal or excellent? Would you hire someone who is pleasant to work with and lights up the room when they walk in, or would you hire someone who sucks the energy out of the environment? Would you hire someone who begs you for a job, or someone whose work is indicative of the level of preparation for the job? Consider the viewpoint of the person you are seeking to work for when preparing for your next audition.

Back to the meeting I mentioned earlier.

During my meeting, I asked this young actress how her career was progressing, and she told me, "Not very well." She then asked me, "What does it take to succeed?"

I paused, turned the question around, and asked her the following: "What have you done in the past thirty days to improve your skills? What have you read? What acting classes have you taken? What film shorts have you created? What are you doing to maximizing your chances of success?"

She then realized that she was not working as hard to ensure her success. I challenge you to ask and answer those questions every thirty days. Every month, write the answers down. (At this point, you should have a journal for all the writing I have you doing! But also know, if it's not written, it's not true.)

You Booked

Congrats! You booked your first role, feature, or episodic—pat yourself on the back. The first rule in success is to continue to do what you did to get you there. Don't change a thing. Actually, do more. Practice the same. Practice more. Don't let up.

Also, take that success and invest in yourself. Invest by putting more into your skill sets. One thing money does, if you're wise, is to give you access to increased time. Use that time wisely by identifying areas of expansion. The most significant investment you can make is in you. Do so!

Build out your team. You should now be seeking out a manager, if you are ready for one, and quite possibly a publicist to help establish your brand and establish a name for yourself. Again, this may happen over an extended period, but don't worry, when it does, it will be worth it!

CHAPTER 7
BE SOCIAL

The entertainment business, like all others, is a relationship game. It's who you know and who knows you. So, outside of working on improving your skills, you must also work on your relationships. To that end, attend actor meet–ups, area SAG-AFTRA meetings, and join an organization of other actors. Don't get overly frustrated by not having access to a specific person. You will get access once you get to a certain skill level.

By the way, if you are an actor and you are SAG eligible, work to become a member. Membership has its privileges, and you are not likely to advance your career without joining.

Attend casting workshops, after-hours, and mixers while you immerse yourself in your goals and objectives. The social component is just as critical as the developmental component.

Attend every industry event that you can. Build relationships. All relationships are based on mutual respect. If a producer, director, or representative is violative, then don't deal with them. That may be a tough thing to say, but in today's era, I want to be precise. Relationships, like values and mores, are an individual's choosing. I know of some people who will do anything to make it. ANYTHING.

And I'm not here to evaluate your decision-making, but some people may seek to abuse their power and manipulate you. You will have to arrive at your own decision as to how to interact with them.

I share a story without naming the producer. Ultimately, it is not one of volition but one of power. But the underlying point remains the same.

I had a client who once had been offered a bit part in a studio film. Internally, we were excited about the role, but the money was meager, especially for the client's stature. I had been pushing the producer's partner to increase my client's fee.

The named producer called my client directly and said, "It's okay to pass on this project."

When I was made aware of such, I emailed the named producer regarding the matter. I asked her, in respectful but professional terms, not to violate industry protocol by contacting my client directly, especially in the middle of a negotiation, and indeed for someone she did not personally know.

The named producer then changed the script, eliminated the part, called my client again directly to inform him of such, and then sent me an email, essentially saying that she could do what she wanted to do.

I realized then that person, albeit friendly in our prior personal interactions, had quite the ego, or had been treated poorly by other industry executives before her level of success. Or thought so highly of herself that she thought little of others.

That leads to another point.

The other side of the coin from manifesting failure is internalizing and projecting arrogance. Once you achieve success, you start to treat people who don't have as much notoriety or stature as you less than decent. There are enough notable examples of both for me not to go into further detail, but beware of both. They are equally dangerous.

To be sure, the named producer's success is admirable. However, I operate off mutual respect. And if a person does not respect you, they will not treat you properly in any relationship. People will only treat you how you allow them to treat you. Demand respect.

I heard Shawn Carter say this on *The Breakfast Club* relative to a famous actor he had gotten into a very public quarrel with, and he is correct. Deal with people for who they are and how they behave, not for *what* they do, their title or profession, that is. You may lose projects, or then again, you may gain the one that is right for you!

That's my philosophy and operating basis. You will have to identify yours.

CHAPTER 8
AND THE WINNER IS . . .

> *You have to go through an evolution to get to a place of comfort. You have to go through profound internal hardships.*
>
> —Brad Pitt

The journey to success is not comfortable. The success principles are simple. But the road is not easy.

There will be difficult moments. If you push through those moments, you will grow.

The most important aspect of the journey toward improving your career is you. It is not your contacts. Not your relatives or your coaches. Not your manager or even your agent.

Those entities will aid your career, but at the beginning and the end, it starts and stops with you.

I can't overemphasize this point.

If you are getting overwhelmed or you have reached a point of frustration, reach out to someone whom you trust and respect.

Or, liaise with me via social media. I am here to help.

Another critical consideration to winning is you must create value for your art. It must be of high quality. You have to ensure that whoever is consuming your art receives the benefits. The benefits are an intrinsic exchange for the consumption of your art.

I'll share a story with you about Jamie Foxx. I once hired him to host an event during the 2019 NBA All-Star weekend. He was supposed to appear only for an hour. He stayed two and a half hours and entertained guests to no end. That's the kind of guy he is. He is where he is not only because he is immensely talented, but also because he delivers *value in abundance*. Use *that* as the litmus test.

In closing, during this journey, you may uncover that you no longer want to pursue acting as a career, and that is fine too. One of the things I understand is that the principles of success are transferrable. Work ethic, preparation, and commitment are skill sets that will help you achieve your goals, whatever they are.

The fact of the matter is as long as you're pursuing your goals, the winner is you!

Believe that. And know that I'm rooting for you and your success. Good luck!

RECOMMENDED READS

The Alchemist by Paulo Coelho

Art by L. Ron Hubbard*

Atlas Shrugged by Ayn Rand

The Art of Seduction by Robert Greene

Confessions of a Casting Director by Jen Rudin

Jack: Straight from the Gut by Jack Welch

More Than Enough by Elaine Welteroth**

Movie Speak by Tony Bill

Think and Grow Rich by Napoleon Hill

The New Business of Acting by Brad Lemack

Powerhouse: The Untold Story of Hollywood Agency Creative Artists Agency by James Andrew Miller

Small Screen, Big Picture by Chad Gervich★★★

★This is a must-read for any actor. The exercises on page 112 will help turn you into a pro.

★★This book is a noteworthy example of pure determination and self-love. Emulate it.

★★★The most comprehensive book on the entertainment business you could ever own.

RECOMMENDED PODCASTS

The Mastery Sessions by Robin Sharma

How I Built This with Guy Raz

WEBSITES

privoscapital.com/about-privos-capital

Spend a day reading their website. It is beyond moving.

ABOUT THE AUTHOR

Arthur G. Smith is an entertainment professional with more than fifteen years of experience in the industry. As the founder and president of AGS Media, Inc., a talent management firm for creatives, personalities, and brands, Arthur makes it his mission to bring great artists and their work to the public. In his role as a talent manager, Arthur has managed many leading personalities in film and television, including Deborah Riley Draper, Erica Ash, RonReaco Lee, and Jessie T. Usher. His brand management experience includes managing celebrity engagement for such clients as Chrysler, PepsiCo, State Farm, and AT&T, working with Anthony Anderson, Jamie Foxx, Taraji P. Henson, Tracee Ellis Ross, Jussie Smollett, and Terrence J.

Arthur founded the Entertainment Marketing Special Interest Group (SIG)—the first of its kind in the seventy-one-year history of the Atlanta chapter of the American Marketing Association (AMA). He also served as creative consultant for the development of Adly, the celebrity advertising tech platform.

An alumnus of both North Carolina A&T State University (where he was elected student body president) and the University of Missouri–Kansas City, Arthur remains an avid long-distance runner and a Circle member of the

High Museum of Art. An Atlanta native and resident, he is the proud father of Khalid, a student at the University of Southern California.

For news and alerts from Arthur G. Smith, visit his social media:

@arthurgsmith
@theactorsguidetosuccess
@powertalkventures

To inquire about booking Arthur G. Smith for a speaking engagement, please contact AGS Media, Inc., at bookings@agsmediainc.com.

Thank you for purchasing and reading this book. And I genuinely hope that it impacted your life as a creative. If you want to get in touch with me to share a success story, or if you have additional questions, I'd love to hear from you!

AGS Media, Inc.
245 N. Highland Ave. Suite 230-523
Atlanta, GA 30307
USA

www.ingramcontent.com/pod-product-compliance
Lightning Source LLC
Chambersburg PA
CBHW061434050726
47593CB00006B/2345